CW01149742

Original title:
Garden of Us

Copyright © 2024 Swan Charm
All rights reserved.

Author: Daisy Dewi
ISBN HARDBACK: 978-9908-1-2725-5
ISBN PAPERBACK: 978-9908-1-2726-2
ISBN EBOOK: 978-9908-1-2727-9

Leaves of Legacy

Amidst the trees, the whispers flow,
Stories of times, both high and low.
Each leaf a tale, in colors bright,
A dance of seasons, both day and night.

Rooted in earth, their bonds hold tight,
Echoes of strength, through every plight.
The gentle rustle, a soothing sound,
In legacy's arms, we are all found.

A Canopy of Togetherness

Under the boughs, we gather near,
A haven of love, a place sincere.
Branches entwined, a shelter strong,
In unity's warmth, we all belong.

With laughter shared and secrets told,
A tapestry rich, in hues of gold.
Each moment cherished, in nature's hold,
A canopy bright, a story bold.

Weaving Nature's Affection

In every petal, a soft embrace,
Nature's kindness leaves a trace.
Threads of green in the gentle breeze,
Weaving a bond with grace and ease.

The rivers murmur, the mountains sigh,
In harmony's song, we learn to fly.
Every bloom, a fragrant prayer,
A promise of love, hanging in the air.

A Canopy of Togetherness

Under the boughs, we gather near,
A haven of love, a place sincere.
Branches entwined, a shelter strong,
In unity's warmth, we all belong.

With laughter shared and secrets told,
A tapestry rich, in hues of gold.
Each moment cherished, in nature's hold,
A canopy bright, a story bold.

Weaving Nature's Affection

In every petal, a soft embrace,
Nature's kindness leaves a trace.
Threads of green in the gentle breeze,
Weaving a bond with grace and ease.

The rivers murmur, the mountains sigh,
In harmony's song, we learn to fly.
Every bloom, a fragrant prayer,
A promise of love, hanging in the air.

The Moment Between the Blooms

Between the blooms, a silence sings,
A pause of peace, where nature clings.
Soft shadows fall, in muted light,
Breath held tight in the still of night.

In that fleeting, tranquil space,
Life holds its breath, a gentle grace.
Awaiting the burst of colors bright,
The moment blooms, then takes to flight.

Petals on the Breeze

Gentle whispers float along,
Carried softly, sweet and strong.
A dance of colors in the air,
Beauty blooms with every care.

Each petal tells a silent tale,
Of sunshine, rain, and stormy gales.
They twirl and swirl, a fleeting grace,
Nature's art in every space.

From garden beds to open fields,
The touch of spring, a joy it yields.
In the breeze, they turn and spin,
A symphony where dreams begin.

As seasons change, they drift away,
Yet memories of their hues will stay.
In every heart, their essence thrives,
A reminder of our joyful lives.

So chase the petals, let them guide,
Through life's journey, side by side.
In their flight, we find our lease,
Among the whispers, find our peace.

The Essence of Collaboration

In the heart of every team,
Lies a spirit, a shared dream.
Together we rise, together we stand,
With strength and unity, hand in hand.

Voices blend in harmony,
Creating paths for all to see.
Ideas spark and visions soar,
One heartbeat, forevermore.

Challenges faced, we won't back down,
Wearing trust like a golden crown.
Each heartbeat syncs, a steady flow,
Together we learn, together we grow.

Respect and kindness light our way,
Celebrating wins along the fray.
With every step, a joy we find,
The essence of collaboration, intertwined.

In the canvas of our shared designs,
A masterpiece in every line.
We write a story, rich and bright,
In collaboration, we find our light.

We Are as One Flower

In a garden vast and wide,
We bloom together, side by side.
Each petal unique, yet we align,
A tapestry of soul, divine.

With colors vibrant, we all show,
A brilliance that continues to grow.
United in purpose, hand in hand,
Together we flourish, take a stand.

From roots entwined beneath the earth,
Springs forth joy, and love, and worth.
Through storms and sun, we find a way,
To blossom bright, come what may.

As one flower, we face the day,
In unity, we find our way.
With fragrance sweet and beauty rare,
A symbol of hope we choose to share.

So let us dance beneath the skies,
In the light of love, we shall rise.
In every heart's embrace, we say,
We are as one, come what may.

Sunshine in Our Souls

A golden glow at break of dawn,
Illuminates the world upon.
With each ray, a promise bright,
Filling hearts with warmth and light.

Through shadows deep and trails unknown,
The sunshine whispers we're not alone.
In every laugh, in every tear,
Its gentle touch brings solace near.

Life's journey filled with ups and downs,
Yet every sorrow wears a crown.
For in our depths, a light resides,
Guiding us through turbulent tides.

Cherish the moments, let them unfold,
In the warmth of sunshine, stories told.
Together we shine, in every role,
Finding joy, sunshine in our souls.

So let it glow, let it be bright,
In every heart, a spark ignites.
Through every challenge, we will stroll,
Forever bright, sunshine in our souls.

The Rich Soil of Shared Dreams

In the garden where hopes lie,
Seeds of visions intertwined.
Watered by laughter and care,
Together we cultivate the sky.

Hands shall reach beneath the earth,
Nurturing dreams as they bloom.
With each whisper, a new rebirth,
We create life, dispelling gloom.

The sun smiles upon our toil,
Fruits of labor, rich and sweet.
In unity, we find our soil,
Harvesting joy, oh how complete!

Beneath the stars, we stand proud,
Sharing in blessings that we've sown.
In this moment, we are loud,
Our ambitions have truly grown.

So let us weave our dreams as one,
In this fertile ground we stand.
Together, brighter than the sun,
Creating futures, hand in hand.

Sunlight through Our Togetherness

Sunrise colors fill the sky,
Warming hearts as shadows flee.
In the morning light, we fly,
Together, we are wild and free.

Hands entwined, we walk the path,
Every step, a joyous song.
Through the giggles and the laughs,
Together is where we belong.

As clouds drift, so do our fears,
Chasing moments, bright and new.
In the warmth of shared frontiers,
Love's embrace always pulls us through.

With each heartbeat, we shine bright,
Illuminating life's great dance.
In unity, we find our light,
Painting dreams with every glance.

So let your spirit rise and play,
In the sunlight, we will grow.
With togetherness, each day,
We spread love's gentle glow.

Dancing Shadows on Evening Grass

The sun dips low, a golden hue,
Shadows stretch across the ground.
In twilight's arms, I dance with you,
In every movement, love is found.

Each rustle whispers ancient songs,
Carried on the cool night air.
We twirl and laugh, where we belong,
In this moment, free from care.

Fireflies flicker, stars ignite,
Guiding our steps with their light.
In the stillness of the night,
Our hearts beat bold, spirits in flight.

Each gentle breeze, a soft caress,
The earth beneath, a sacred space.
Together, our worries recess,
In evening's glow, we find our grace.

So let's sway 'neath the moon's soft glow,
In this dance, our spirits soar.
With every step, love will flow,
As shadows play forevermore.

The Language of Quiet Growth

In silence, the seeds take root,
Beneath the surface, life abounds.
With patience, we witness the shoot,
Emerging slowly from dark grounds.

Each moment, a lesson unfolds,
In whispers of nature's design.
With each heartbeat, the story holds,
The strength of roots intertwine.

Listen close to the gentle earth,
Where dreams are nurtured from our pain.
In stillness lies a sacred birth,
In unity, growth remains.

Time teaches with tender grace,
In quietude, we discover.
Every journey finds its place,
As we bloom, we've so much to cover.

So let us honor the quiet ways,
In every leaf, in every breath.
In the beauty of subtle days,
Together we rise, defying death.

Secret Paths of Us

In hidden trails where whispers dwell,
We wander softly, hearts compelled.
Silence speaks of dreams we chase,
In secret paths, we find our place.

Through tangled roots, our bond we weave,
In every glance, the love conceived.
The shadows dance, the moonlight glows,
Together still, our story grows.

With every step, the world turns bright,
In stolen hours, we embrace the night.
With every heartbeat, truths emerge,
In secret paths, our souls converge.

Beneath the stars, our laughter sings,
In gentle winds, the freedom brings.
Together now, through all that's new,
On secret paths, it's me and you.

As morning light breaks through the trees,
We trace the lines of memories.
In every sigh, a promise lasts,
On secret paths, we'll walk steadfast.

Ferns of Fidelity

Amidst the green, where ferns arise,
We nurture love, a bond so wise.
In gentle shades, our hearts align,
In ferns of faith, our souls entwine.

Each leaf a story, vibrant, true,
In every touch, the old and new.
Together through life's winding way,
In ferns of fidelity, here we stay.

The rain may fall, the storms may roar,
Yet side by side, we'll weather more.
In every challenge, trust expands,
In ferns of love, we take our stands.

Soft whispers fill the air we share,
In every moment, love's sweet care.
With roots so deep, and branches high,
In ferns of fidelity, we soar the sky.

As time moves on, our spirits thrive,
In nature's arms, we feel alive.
Together strong, through laughter's sound,
In ferns of fidelity, our hearts are bound.

In the Shade of Togetherness

Beneath the trees, where shadows play,
We find our peace, day by day.
In gentle whispers, warmth unfolds,
In the shade of us, a story told.

With hands entwined, the world fades out,
In quiet moments, we share no doubt.
In every sigh, where comfort reigns,
In the shade of togetherness, love remains.

The sun may shine, yet here we stay,
In sheltering arms, we gently sway.
With laughter bright, our worries cease,
In the shade of togetherness, we find peace.

Through seasons change, our roots run deep,
In bonds of love, we never leap.
Together strong, through thick and thin,
In the shade of us, our lives begin.

As twilight falls, our hearts align,
In every heartbeat, your soul and mine.
Within this space, forever blessed,
In the shade of togetherness, we are at rest.

Encounters Among the Blossoms

In gardens bright, where flowers bloom,
Our paths collide, dispelling gloom.
With every glance, a spark ignites,
Among the blossoms, our love ignites.

Each petal soft, a tender kiss,
In fragrant air, we find our bliss.
Together wandering, hand in hand,
Among the blossoms, we make our stand.

The colors dance, as hearts collide,
In playful breezes, we take our stride.
With each encounter, the world transforms,
Among the blossoms, we weather storms.

As laughter rings through perfumed air,
In moments brief, we find our prayer.
With blossoms sweet, our spirits soar,
Among the blossoms, we seek for more.

As seasons pass, the memories grow,
In every petal, love's gentle glow.
Together still, in life's sweet trust,
Among the blossoms, it's me and us.

Our Blooming Odyssey

In fields where wildflowers sway,
We dance as the sun greets day.
With every step, we find our way,
In this odyssey, hearts at play.

Eyes bright with dreams untold,
We chase the warmth, the hopes of gold.
Through shadows deep and stories bold,
Our spirits soar, forever hold.

Each petal whispers secrets sweet,
Beneath our feet, the earth's heartbeat.
Together we rise, never to retreat,
In this journey, love's perfect feat.

Threads of Gold in Greenery

Amidst the leaves, the sunlight gleams,
We weave through life, as nature dreams.
In emerald hues, our laughter streams,
Binding us close, in golden seams.

Each moment stitched with gentle grace,
In the fabric of time, we find our place.
With every thread, we interlace,
Together, love's warm embrace.

The rustle of leaves, a soft caress,
In every heartbeat, we feel it's blessed.
In this tapestry, we are expressed,
Threads of gold, in life's finesse.

Whispers in the Underbrush

In the underbrush, secrets creep,
Where shadows linger, silence deep.
Soft whispers of the night we keep,
Nature's lullaby, a calming leap.

Beneath the stars, we softly tread,
With every murmur, our spirits fed.
In the dark, where dreams are spread,
Here lies the path, where fears are shed.

Glimmers of light through tangled vines,
A dance of shadows, the heart aligns.
In whispers, we find the stars that shine,
Nature's secrets, forever divine.

The Seasons of Your Laughter

In springtime blooms, your laughter rings,
A melody born with blossoming things.
In vibrant hues, joy always clings,
Your smile ignites what each season brings.

Summer's sun, it's warm embrace,
We share our hopes in a golden space.
With every glance, love leaves a trace,
In the warmth of your laughter's grace.

Autumn leaves fall, a soft goodbye,
Yet in your laughter, I see the sky.
In hues of amber, we learn to fly,
With every chuckle, our spirits high.

Winter blankets with snowy delight,
Your laughter sparkles, a beacon bright.
Through frosty nights, you are my light,
In every season, love takes flight.

Flourishing in Each Other's Light

In shadows cast, we find our way,
Each whisper soft, each glance a ray.
Together we bloom, our roots entwined,
In every heartbeat, love aligned.

Through storms that shake, we stand as one,
Reaching for warmth, we bask in sun.
With every dawn, new colors rise,
In each other's light, we touch the skies.

Serenade of the Soil

Beneath the earth, the secrets hum,
In gentle whispers, they sway and strum.
Roots intertwine, a hidden song,
Where every note makes us belong.

From seed to bloom, the journey's sweet,
In nature's arms, our hearts do meet.
Together we grow, in sun and rain,
A serenade that eases pain.

Petal-Paved Pathways

With every step on paths of bloom,
We leave behind the past's dull gloom.
Petals scatter, a vibrant trace,
In every corner, love's embrace.

We wander wide, hand in hand,
On trails where dreams and joys expand.
Through fragrant fields, we find our way,
In petal-paved paths, we choose to stay.

The Rhythm of Shared Seasons

As winter whispers, we draw near,
In cozy corners, we hold dear.
With spring, we dance in colors bright,
Each shared moment, pure delight.

Summer brings warmth, laughter's song,
In golden days, we both belong.
When autumn leaves begin to fall,
We share the beauty, through it all.

Confetti of Wildflower Wishes

In fields where wildflowers dance,
Dreams take flight in vibrant chance.
Colors swirl like laughter's sound,
Nature's joy all around.

Each petal whispers soft delight,
Wishes carried on the light.
Hearts connect in gentle sway,
A tapestry of bright bouquet.

Breezes play a sweet refrain,
Echoes of a summer's gain.
In this moment, spirits soar,
A glimpse of what we all adore.

With every wish released to bloom,
Life's canvas bursts beyond the gloom.
Confetti strewn across the day,
In nature's grand ballet.

A Canvas of Cherished Time

Each moment brushed with golden hue,
Capturing dreams, both old and new.
Memories painted, bold and bright,
A canvas dancing in the light.

Time flows like rivers in the night,
Each stroke a whisper, pure delight.
Moments framed with joy and tears,
Layers soft, through all the years.

Brushstrokes render shadows long,
Echoes of a silent song.
In colors that our hearts recall,
A masterpiece that binds us all.

With every glance, a story told,
Of love that blossoms, brave and bold.
A canvas where our hearts entwine,
In the tapestry of time.

Blossoming Memories In Sunlight

Sunlight spills on morning dew,
Whispers of the past break through.
Each ray a glimmer, soft and warm,
Embracing us in nature's charm.

Blossoms open, stories grow,
Memories drift like petals flow.
Captured in a tranquil pause,
Time stands still without a cause.

Laughter echoes through the trees,
Carried gently on the breeze.
Golden hours weave their thread,
In the light where dreams are fed.

Shade and sun in sweet embrace,
Nature's dance, a sacred space.
Blossoming in this bright delight,
Memories bloom in morning light.

The Serenity of Tender Roots

Beneath the earth, the roots entwine,
In silent strength, their prayers align.
Whispers from the ground ascend,
A tranquil bond they choose to tend.

Cradled in the soil's soft care,
Life's energy flows, bright and rare.
The past connects with what's to come,
In nature's dance, we all succumb.

Branches reach for endless skies,
While deep below, the spirit lies.
In tender love, we find our peace,
And from these roots, our joys increase.

Together growing, side by side,
The strength of family, love, and pride.
In every leaf, a story blooms,
The serenity of roots consumes.

Intertwined in Verdant Bliss

In the garden where we meet,
Nature hums a gentle tune.
Roots entwined beneath our feet,
Dancing under the silver moon.

Every leaf a whispering dream,
Branches stretch towards the sky.
In sunlight, our spirits beam,
Together, we learn to fly.

The breeze carries our laughter,
Petals soft beneath our touch.
In this moment, ever after,
We bloom, holding on so much.

Amidst the verdant hue we sway,
Our hearts sync in gentle rhythm.
Every dawn, anew we play,
In this blissful garden prism.

The Nature of Our Togetherness

Two rivers flow, side by side,
With currents strong yet serene.
In harmony, we must abide,
For in union, we are seen.

Mountains rise, steadfast and bold,
A fortress for our whispered dreams.
In shadows, stories unfold,
Bound together, or so it seems.

Whispers of the woods surround,
Echoes of our shared delight.
In every sound, our love is found,
Illuminated in starlit night.

With each step upon this Earth,
We weave the fabric of our days.
Celebrating our shared worth,
In the sunlight's warming rays.

Wildflowers of Connection

Amidst the fields, wildflowers bloom,
Bright colors in a gentle sway.
Each petal holds a sweet perfume,
Marking love in nature's play.

In scattered sunlight, we entwine,
Dancing on the gentle breeze.
Hearts aligned like nature's design,
In this bliss, we find our ease.

The roots beneath us intertwined,
A tapestry of vibrant grace.
In every glance, our hearts aligned,
In this wildflower embrace.

We are the songs of bees in flight,
A chorus of the sun and rain.
Together, we ignite the light,
In the wild, we break the chain.

Sweet Fragrance of Together

Fragrant blooms in morning's light,
A melody that fills the air.
With every touch, our hearts ignite,
In this garden, love is rare.

Petals painted with golden hue,
We breathe in the warmth of our fate.
Each moment spent feels fresh and new,
In the arms of love, we create.

As twilight drapes the sky with stars,
We find solace in the night.
Bound together, no more scars,
In the love that feels so right.

With every fragrance, we unveil,
The beauty of our tender bond.
In this world, we will prevail,
In sweet togetherness, we're fond.

Nectar of Our Hidden Moments

In whispers sweet, we share our dreams,
Beneath the shade, where sunlight beams.
Every glance, a story told,
In silent vows, our hearts unfold.

Like morning dew on petals bright,
We savor days, from dark to light.
In secret spaces, time stands still,
Each breath a promise, love's true thrill.

The laughter dances in the air,
A gentle bond, a tender care.
With every moment, life's embrace,
We taste the nectar, find our place.

In fleeting hours, we intertwine,
With every heartbeat, your hand in mine.
Together weaving, a tapestry,
Of hidden joys, just you and me.

Amidst the rush, we pause to see,
The beauty held in simplicity.
In quiet corners, love does bloom,
Forever sealed in each small room.

Starlit Conversations

Under the canvas of midnight's glow,
We share our thoughts, let feelings flow.
With words like stars, we craft our fate,
In starlit dreams, we elevate.

In the hush of night, our voices rise,
A symphony of truths, no disguise.
Each shared secret, a sparkling gem,
In the universe, it's just us, them.

Questions soar like comets fast,
We cling to moments, make them last.
With laughter soft as the evening breeze,
In this sacred space, our hearts find ease.

The cosmos listens, a witness true,
To every hope and wish with you.
Beneath the twinkle of infinite light,
We find our way through the gentle night.

As night unfolds, our souls entwine,
In this embrace, your heart is mine.
Together we weave our dreams on high,
In starlit conversations; we'll never say goodbye.

The Symphony of Growing Together

In every note, a chance to learn,
With every step, our hearts discern.
Through trials faced and joy celebrated,
In life's great dance, we feel elated.

Like rivers flowing, side by side,
Through every twist, we shall abide.
As seasons change, we mold and bloom,
In harmony, we find our room.

Each challenge met, a chord we play,
Together we rise, come what may.
In laughter shared and tears shed too,
The symphony grows, as me and you.

With every heartbeat, echoes strong,
We find our rhythm, where we belong.
In unity, our spirits soar,
A melody sweet, forever more.

With hands entwined, we chart the skies,
Together we build, we dream, we rise.
In this grand symphony, hearts at tether,
With love as our guide, we grow together.

Tapestry of Every Season

In springtime's bloom, we find our start,
With budding leaves and open heart.
Each petal kissed by morning dew,
A promise made, renewed with you.

Summer's warmth, like sunlit smiles,
We dance through days, embrace the miles.
With laughter bright, we paint the skies,
In every sunset, love never dies.

As autumn whispers, leaves turn gold,
We gather stories, both new and old.
In cozy corners, hearts align,
In every moment, our lives intertwine.

Winter's chill may frost the air,
But in our hearts, it's love we share.
Through every storm, we brave the night,
In each other's arms, we find our light.

With threads of joy and strands of pain,
We weave our lives in sun and rain.
In every season, through thoughts profound,
The tapestry grows, forever bound.

Our Shared Oasis

In the heart of a desert wide,
We found a spring to abide.
Beneath the palms, we rest and sway,
A tranquil place where we can play.

Whispers dance upon the breeze,
Carrying secrets among the trees.
We sip from the well of our dreams,
Life is richer than it seems.

Footprints left upon the sand,
Mark the journey, hand in hand.
Together we cultivate this space,
In our oasis, we embrace.

Stars above like diamonds shine,
Illuminating your hand in mine.
The night wraps us in its fold,
As stories of our hearts unfold.

Here in our haven, we stand tall,
Through each rise, through every fall.
In the garden of life we grow,
Nourished by love's gentle glow.

A Symphony of Growing Together

In harmony, our lives entwine,
Each note a story, yours and mine.
With every chord, we build our song,
Melodies sweet where we belong.

We share the struggle, share the strife,
Together composing the song of life.
From silent whispers to a bold refrain,
Our voices echo through joy and pain.

The rhythms shift, the tempo swells,
In sync, we write our tales to tell.
United hearts, a canvas bright,
Painting the world in pure delight.

Through crescendos and soft declines,
We find ourselves in the tangled lines.
Trusting the beats and the breaths we take,
In this symphony, we won't break.

So let the music play on strong,
With every heartbeat, we belong.
In the orchestra of our lives,
Together is where the magic thrives.

The Intermingling of Souls

In the tapestry of life we weave,
Threads of gold and silver leave.
Winding closely, side by side,
In each other, we confide.

Like rivers meeting in the sea,
Your essence flows into me.
Bridging gaps that once seemed wide,
Together, we let love decide.

Laughter mingles with tender sighs,
Underneath the endless skies.
Moments merge, our spirits blend,
In unity, we find our end.

Through the trials, through the grace,
In this dance, we find our place.
A rhythm gentle, hearts aligned,
In this love, forever entwined.

So let us cherish every part,
Of this beautiful work of art.
In every glance, in every role,
We celebrate the intermingling soul.

Sunbeams and Shared Smiles

In the glow of the morning light,
Sunbeams dance, warm and bright.
Your laughter rings like chimes in air,
A sweet reminder that we care.

Through fields of flowers, we roam free,
The beauty of life, just you and me.
With every smile, our spirits soar,
Creating memories we'll adore.

As shadows fade, hope ignites,
Together we chase the beautiful sights.
Every moment, a gift to claim,
In the sunshine, we feel no shame.

Hand in hand, we walk this path,
Embracing joy, avoiding wrath.
With shared smiles, we light the way,
In this journey, come what may.

So let us bask in what we find,
In every sunbeam, love aligned.
With laughter echoing through the miles,
We are forever, sunbeams and smiles.

Unity in Every Leaf

In the whisper of a breeze, we find,
Leaves rustle in harmony, intertwined.
Each green speaks of stories rare,
Together they breathe, a bond they share.

Underneath the ancient oak's embrace,
Roots dig deep, they hold their place.
Branches reaching, they touch the skies,
In unity, their strength defies.

Raindrops fall, a gentle song,
Nature's choir, where we belong.
From the smallest bud to the tallest tree,
In every leaf, united, we see.

Seasons change, yet they remain,
In the dance of life, joy and pain.
Together they weather sun and storm,
In unity, they take on form.

So let us learn from each green leaf,
In togetherness, find our belief.
Through every trial, hand in hand,
In unity's grace, we forever stand.

Soft Shadows of Companionship

In quiet corners where we sit,
Silhouettes dance, soft and lit.
Laughter floats like a gentle sigh,
Companions wrapped in twilight's dye.

The world outside may lose its voice,
But in each other, we rejoice.
With shared secrets, hearts unfold,
Soft shadows cast stories told.

Together we weave moments bright,
In each flicker of fading light.
Hand in hand, we brave the night,
Soft shadows guide us to what feels right.

With every whisper, trust is grown,
In the silence, love is shown.
In the warmth of friendship's grace,
Soft shadows call us to this place.

So let us walk through this dreamland,
In soft shadows, forever stand.
For in companionship, we find our way,
With hearts together, come what may.

Melodies of Nature's Kinship

The brook hums a timeless tune,
While the sun greets the afternoon.
Birds chirp in a sweet refrain,
Nature's kinship, a soft domain.

Leaves rustle in a gentle choir,
Each note stirs the heart's desire.
The wind carries whispers of the past,
In melodies, memories are cast.

Mountain peaks echo tales from afar,
Underneath the twinkling star.
Every creature, every tree,
Plays its part in harmony.

In the fields, the flowers sway,
Their colors dance, in joyous play.
Together they paint the evening's glow,
In nature's song, our spirits grow.

So listen close, let your heart sing,
In every breeze, life's offerings.
Melodies of kinship rise above,
In nature's arms, we find true love.

Petal-Soft Conversations

In gardens bright where petals lie,
Soft whispers bloom beneath the sky.
Butterflies flit with stories sweet,
In petal-soft chats, our hearts meet.

Every color, a voice so clear,
In gentle tones, we draw near.
Through fragrant air, secrets abound,
In every petal, a truth is found.

The morning dew, a shared delight,
In the warmth of day, our dreams take flight.
Breezes carry words unspoken,
In petal-soft bonds, each heart's not broken.

As twilight falls in hues of gold,
The stories of blossoms begin to unfold.
With every chat, new friendships grow,
In gardens of care, we let love flow.

So linger here, in nature's space,
Let petals tell us of love's embrace.
In soft conversations of the day,
Together we find our own way.

Nature's Tapestry of Us

In the forest, whispers of leaves,
Breezes carry stories we weave.
Mossy paths beneath our feet,
Every heartbeat feels complete.

Sunlight dances on the stream,
Every shadow, a shared dream.
Birds sing songs of joy and grace,
In this wild, we find our place.

Mountains rise, ancient and wise,
Holding secrets in the skies.
With every star that softly glows,
Nature's love forever flows.

In the garden, colors blend,
Petals whisper, hearts they mend.
Hand in hand through blooms we roam,
Every petal feels like home.

Seasons change, yet still we grow,
Roots entwined in earth below.
In this tapestry of trust,
Together, we are one with dust.

Echoes in the Blooming Space

Petals flutter in gentle sway,
Echoes linger where children play.
Sunrise whispers soft and clear,
Filling hearts with gentle cheer.

In the meadow, colors bright,
Joyful echoes take to flight.
Every breeze shares tales untold,
Promises in blooms unfold.

Butterflies kiss the morning light,
Dancing softly, pure delight.
Every fragrance, blissful sigh,
In this bloom, our spirits fly.

Over hills, the shadows stretch,
Nature's beauty, dreams bequeath.
In every blossom, hope is found,
In every heart, love knows no bound.

So let us wander, hand in hand,
Through blooming spaces, hearts expand.
In this echo, forever bright,
We find joy in shared light.

The Colors of Our Belonging

In vibrant hues, our stories blend,
Upon this canvas, hearts transcend.
Every shade, a voice, a song,
In unity, we all belong.

Like the sunset, warm and bold,
Each moment shared, a treasure told.
Through laughter's glow and tears' embrace,
In these colors, we find our place.

Brushstrokes tender, timid yet free,
Mingling dreams that long to be.
With every heartbeat, every sigh,
We paint our world with love's sweet cry.

The morning light breaks through the haze,
Illuminating our joyful days.
In this tapestry of ties so strong,
We find the notes to life's great song.

So let each color rise and sing,
Of the love and peace we bring.
Together in this vibrant throng,
In life's gallery, we all belong.

Twilight in the Flowerbed

As twilight falls, the world aglow,
In the flowerbed, time moves slow.
Petals close, whispering goodnight,
Stars awaken, bringing light.

Crickets chirp a serenade,
Underneath the willow's shade.
Night unfolds her velvet cape,
In the garden, dreams escape.

Moonlight bathes each bloom in grace,
Soft reflections, a tender embrace.
In the silence, hearts connect,
In this moment, love we reflect.

A gentle breeze through leaves will sweep,
As shadows gather, secrets keep.
In this space, the night is ours,
Amongst the whispers of the stars.

So let us linger, hand in hand,
Where every flower makes its stand.
In the twilight's soothing breath,
We find our peace, we conquer death.

Whispers Beneath the Petals

In the garden where shadows play,
Soft secrets dance on a breeze today.
Petals flutter, secrets shared,
Nature's whispers, tenderly declared.

Beneath the blooms, stories hide,
Of fleeting moments, hearts collide.
With each sigh, the flowers sway,
Offering hope in a gentle way.

Sunlight dapples the vibrant hue,
Every color tells a truth anew.
In silence, dreams begin to spin,
As nature's chorus draws us in.

A fragrant breeze wraps us tight,
In the embrace of soft twilight.
Listen closely, the petals hum,
A melody of all we've become.

Beneath the stars, the petals glow,
Illuminating the love we sow.
In whispers soft, our hearts unite,
A bond as lasting as the night.

The Bloom of Our Secrets

In every corner, silence thrives,
Where buried truths begin to rise.
A petal's blush, a shared desire,
Our hidden thoughts ignite a fire.

In the stillness, dreams unfold,
Secrets shimmer, tales retold.
With every breath, we find our way,
Through blossoming hopes in disarray.

Petals whisper, closely tied,
In the garden where love resides.
The fragrance speaks of what we've known,
In the silence, our hearts have grown.

As colors merge, our fears take flight,
In the garden, everything feels right.
Each bloom a promise, soft and sweet,
In the shadows, our lives meet.

Under starlit skies we stand,
Bound by secrets, hand in hand.
In each flower, our truths cascade,
Together in this glorious parade.

Tangled Vines of Connection

Twisted paths where silence weaves,
In every heart, a thread that cleaves.
Through tangled vines, our souls entwine,
A network rich, a love divine.

Branches reaching, bending low,
Carrying whispers only we know.
In shaded corners, laughter rings,
With hidden joy, our spirit sings.

Winding roots beneath the ground,
Where strength resides, our hearts are found.
With every touch, we nurture life,
Binding together, husband, wife.

Through storms and sun, we grow and thrive,
In every struggle, love's alive.
Tangled vines, a tapestry,
Together, we become the tree.

Amidst the leaves, our stories flow,
The journeys taken, seeds we sow.
In every twist, our spirits are free,
Forever bound in harmony.

Where Moonlight Meets Dreams

Underneath the silver glow,
Night whispers tales we both know.
With every star, a wish takes flight,
In the stillness, hearts unite.

Moonlit paths guide our way,
Through shadows where dreams softly play.
In the quiet, aspirations gleam,
Where reality melds with every dream.

Beneath the heavens, all is bright,
Where shadows fade and hearts ignite.
In the silence, secrets rise,
Reflected in your loving eyes.

With every pulse, the night expands,
As destiny weaves its gentle strands.
In silver beams, our hopes align,
Together in this cosmic design.

As sleep enfolds, we drift away,
To realms where dreams invite us to stay.
In moonlight's embrace, we are found,
In the dance of dreams, love knows no bound.

The Orchard of Wishes

In the orchard where dreams grow,
Beneath the sun's warm embrace,
Whispers of hope start to flow,
Filling the silent space.

Each blossom holds a secret light,
Bringing forth joy, pure and bright,
Branches sway with gentle grace,
Echoing wishes in this place.

A breeze stirs the petals' dance,
Carrying dreams in every glance,
The earth hums a soft refrain,
Nurturing hopes like gentle rain.

As twilight casts a golden glow,
Stars awaken, one by one,
In the orchard, wishes flow,
Underneath the setting sun.

Each wish a seed, planted deep,
In hearts where memories keep,
The orchard of wishes will thrive,
As long as dreams are alive.

A Symphony of Colors Unfurling

In the canvas of the dawn,
Colors burst, delicate and bright,
Each hue a note gently drawn,
Crafting a symphony of light.

Petals open, soft and sweet,
Nature's orchestra begins to play,
Harmony in every heartbeat,
In the dance of a brand new day.

Cobalt skies and emerald fields,
Gold and crimson intertwine,
A beauty that the earth yields,
Painting a scene divine.

With every brush, a story told,
Of sunsets bright and morning dew,
A tapestry of dreams unfold,
In colors bold, forever true.

So let us stand and take it in,
This symphony that nature sings,
A masterpiece where life begins,
In each colored thread, joy springs.

The Dance of Branches Above

In the gentle breeze they sway,
Whispering secrets to the air,
Branches dance, come what may,
A ballet of nature's care.

Leaves shimmer in the sunlight,
Casting shadows on the ground,
Nature's grace, a pure delight,
In every twist and turn, profound.

An acorn drops with a soft thud,
Landing in a patch of green,
Life begins with just a bud,
In the branches, love is seen.

As seasons change and winds do blow,
The dance remains, a timeless act,
Roots hold firm, while branches flow,
In every movement, life intact.

So look above, the sky adorned,
With a dance of branches bright,
In every sway, a world reborn,
In the dance, we find our light.

The Sweetness of Shared Fragrance

In the garden where blooms meet,
A perfume lingers in the air,
The sweetest scent, a heart's retreat,
In every flower, love laid bare.

Roses blush with tender grace,
Lilies offer solace rare,
Each fragrance finds its rightful place,
Creating moments we can share.

On soft winds, the aromas glide,
Carrying whispers far and wide,
In the hush of twilight's hue,
The sweetness binds me close to you.

Through petaled paths, our laughter flies,
Intertwined with scents divine,
With every breath, a bond that ties,
In the garden, hearts align.

So let us walk where flowers bloom,
And breathe in love, both near and far,
In shared fragrances, dispelling gloom,
Together, we shine like a star.

The Canopy of Us

In the shade where shadows play,
Our dreams intertwine and sway.
Whispers of leaves dance around,
In this haven, love is found.

Beneath the arch of emerald skies,
We share secrets, no disguise.
Sunlight filters through our hearts,
Binding us, never apart.

With every breeze, our spirits soar,
Together, we can be much more.
Branches stretch with hope anew,
Forever held in canopy blue.

And when the storms begin to roar,
We stand strong, through every pour.
Roots entwined, we bear the weight,
Nurturing love that won't abate.

In the twilight, stars will gleam,
Above our dreams, a silver beam.
Underneath this vast expanse,
Our souls entwined in a gentle dance.

Roots Beneath the Surface

Beneath the ground, where shadows creep,
Our story lies, quiet and deep.
Tangled whispers of days gone by,
In the darkness, memories lie.

Crimson roots grasping the earth,
Each one tells of tenderness and mirth.
Nurtured by the rains of time,
Growing stronger, rhythm and rhyme.

In silence, they hold tales untold,
Of summer whispers and winters bold.
They spread wide, like arms in prayer,
Reaching out, everywhere.

Through trials faced and seasons turned,
The bonds we've built, forever earned.
Together, we bloom, strong and true,
Fostering life with every dew.

And when storms rage overhead,
Roots remind us of paths we tread.
For what lies deep is never lost,
In the union, we embrace the cost.

Harvesting Laughter from Dew

In the morn, a glimmering light,
Dewdrops catch the sun so bright.
Laughter drips from petals soft,
As joy unfolds like wings aloft.

Each drop a moment, pure and clear,
Harvesting smiles, banishing fear.
Nature's melody fills the air,
Bringing warmth, beyond compare.

Playful breezes brush our cheeks,
In this bliss, our spirit speaks.
With every giggle, each small sigh,
We claim the day, as time goes by.

Together, we dance in morning's glow,
Chasing shadows, fast and slow.
For in these moments, wild and free,
We plant the seeds of harmony.

As the sun begins to rise,
With every laugh, our hearts will rise.
So let us cherish what we see,
Harvesting joy, you and me.

Silhouettes Beneath the Blossoms

In twilight's hush, we find our place,
Silhouettes soft in nature's embrace.
Petals flutter, a gentle sigh,
As stars awaken in the sky.

Beneath the blooms, our stories blend,
With every breath, the night we send.
Whispers echo, love's sweet refrain,
In this moment, we feel no pain.

Guided by a silver beam,
We wander through this fragrant dream.
Arms entwined, we sway and glide,
In the shadows, love's our guide.

The blossoms drop, a soft cascade,
Cushioning dreams we've gently laid.
In petals' drift, we find our tune,
Serenading beneath the moon.

With every heartbeat, we re-align,
Creating a dance that feels divine.
Together, forever, in the night,
Silhouettes shining, pure and bright.

A Sanctuary of Two Souls

In the quiet of the night, we breathe,
Where whispers linger, and hearts believe.
Two souls entwined, in soft embrace,
Finding solace in this sacred space.

Through storms and trials, we have found,
A sanctuary where love is profound.
With every heartbeat, a promise made,
In this haven, fear will soon fade.

Together we dance beneath the stars,
Healing each other's invisible scars.
Time slows down as we softly soar,
In our haven, we ask for nothing more.

The world outside may grow wild and loud,
But in our sanctuary, we stand proud.
Hand in hand, we face the unknown,
For in each other, we have grown.

So let the winds of change blow free,
In this forever, you and me.
Our love's reflection in the moon's light,
A sanctuary of two souls, shining bright.

Flora of Our Delighted Hearts

In gardens lush, where colors blend,
Flora of love begins to ascend.
With every petal, a story we weave,
Of whispered dreams, hearts that believe.

Sun-kissed blooms in vibrant hues,
Each one a memory we choose.
In fragrant air, our laughter sways,
A dance of joy in sunlit rays.

The daisies nod in a gentle breeze,
While violets bow with elegant ease.
Nature's chorus, our sweetest tune,
In the glow of afternoon.

Through seasons that come, and those that pass,
Our love will flourish, like blades of grass.
Rooted deep, with strength and grace,
Flora of our hearts, a sacred space.

So let us nurture this garden bright,
With tender care and pure delight.
In every blossom, our love shall bloom,
A haven found amid life's room.

Intertwined in Indigo Shadows

In twilight realms where shadows dance,
We found each other, lost in a trance.
Underneath the indigo sky,
Together we breathe, you and I.

Stars awaken, whispers ignite,
In the hush of the softening night.
With secrets shared, our hearts align,
In this sacred space, your hand in mine.

The cool night air, a gentle caress,
In your gaze, I find my rest.
Every glance, a tethered thread,
Intertwined paths, where love is fed.

As shadows merge, we leave the day,
Embraced by night, nothing in the way.
Two souls wandering, side by side,
In this indigo, we shall abide.

With every heartbeat, time stands still,
In this moment, we find our will.
Forever entwined in twilight's hue,
In indigo shadows, just me and you.

Budding Trust in the Twilight

As daylight fades and stars appear,
Budding trust, we quietly endear.
In the twilight's gentle embrace,
We share our thoughts, our sacred space.

With every word, a flower blooms,
Softly dispelling impending glooms.
Open hearts, like petals unfurl,
In the simplicity, we find our world.

Flickers of light guide our way,
In trust's warmth, we choose to stay.
To nurture dreams as the night unfolds,
Together we stand, brave and bold.

In silence deep, we build our trust,
A bond so rich, in love we must.
Every moment, a step we take,
In twilight's glow, our hearts awake.

So let the stars our witness be,
In budding trust, just you and me.
Through the layers of the night,
We find our path, our guiding light.

Sanctuary of Shared Dreams

In whispers soft, we gather here,
Where hopes reside, and sorrows clear.
Beneath the stars, our spirits soar,
A safe embrace, forevermore.

Each laughter shared, a thread we weave,
In unity, we dare believe.
A tapestry of light and grace,
Within these walls, our sacred space.

Through stormy nights, our voices blend,
A harmony that shall not end.
In dreams we share, our hearts align,
This sanctuary, yours and mine.

With open arms, we welcome all,
No soul shall feel the weight of fall.
In quiet moments, we find peace,
A cherished bond that shall not cease.

As dawn breaks through, the world awakes,
In shared dreams, a new path makes.
Together here, we stand as one,
In this haven, life's race is run.

The Blooming Heartbeat

In gardens lush, our hearts do swell,
With petals soft, a tale to tell.
Each bloom a pulse, a rhythm strong,
In nature's dance, we all belong.

As sunlight kisses morning dew,
The vibrant hues ignite anew.
In fragrant whispers, love is found,
A melody that wraps around.

Beneath the skies, our dreams take flight,
With every step, we chase the light.
The bloom of life, a treasured guide,
In this heartbeat, we confide.

Through seasons change, our bond remains,
In laughter sweet, in gentle pains.
A garden nurtured, two hearts meet,
In every petal, love's heartbeat.

So let us dance in moonlight's glow,
With every breath, our passions flow.
In nature's arms, we find our part,
Together, dear, we bloom — our heart.

Secrets Woven in Green

In emerald leaves, our secrets hide,
A world untouched, where dreams abide.
Beneath the boughs, whispers unfold,
In shadows deep, the stories told.

With every breeze, a tale takes flight,
In quiet hush of the shimmering night.
The forest holds our cherished truths,
In soft-lit glades, we taste our youths.

A dance of light through branches sways,
In this embrace, our spirit plays.
With roots entwined, we stand as one,
In nature's grip, our fears undone.

Each rustling leaf, a voice so dear,
In every sound, a song we hear.
Secrets linger, forever bound,
In the lush green, love is found.

So let us roam these sacred trails,
With every step, our spirit sails.
In nature's weave, we find our way,
A tapestry that shall not fray.

Promises Beneath the Canopy

Beneath the shade of ancient trees,
We carve our vows on whispered breeze.
In dappled light, our dreams entwine,
A sacred promise, yours and mine.

With gentle breaths, we share our fears,
In silent oaths, we dry our tears.
The canopy our sheltering guide,
In each soft sigh, love's flame abides.

As shadows dance in twilight's glow,
Our hearts align, a steady flow.
In rustling leaves, our wishes soar,
Together strong, forevermore.

With every heartbeat, we reaffirm,
In nature's arms, our souls will yearn.
Through trials faced, we stand as one,
In whispered promises, love's begun.

So let the world around us fade,
In this sanctuary, unafraid.
With dreams like roots, we grow and thrive,
Beneath the canopy, we come alive.

Raindrops on Shared Leaves

Gentle falls from skies up high,
Whispering breezes softly sigh.
Raindrops dance on emerald green,
Nature's lace, a sight serene.

Cascading sounds in rhythmic flow,
Filling hearts with hopes that glow.
Every drop a fleeting kiss,
Embracing dreams we dare not miss.

The Hidden Pathways We Walk

Beneath the boughs, where shadows play,
Whispers guide us on our way.
Twisting trails, we find our truth,
In every step, reclaim our youth.

Footprints marked on ancient ground,
In silence, deeper joys are found.
Every turn a brand new start,
In this journey, join our heart.

Echoes Among the Blossoms

Petals flutter, colors bright,
Echoes linger in soft light.
Songs of spring fill up the air,
In the garden, love is rare.

Laughter dances on the breeze,
Nature's symphony, hearts at ease.
Chasing dreams on fragrant trails,
In the blooms, our hope prevails.

Fragrant Memories in the Breeze

Summer scents on zephyrs roam,
Tales of laughter, scents of home.
As petals fall, we reminisce,
Moments cherished, purest bliss.

Time may pass, but scents remain,
Whispers linger in sweet refrain.
Each fragrance, a story told,
In the winds, our hearts unfold.

The Color of Our Quiet Reflection

In moments hushed, thoughts intertwine,
Shadows dance in soft twilight shine.
A whisper weaves through the air,
Echoes of silence, tender and rare.

Glimmers of truth in silent streams,
Where our hearts unfold their dreams.
Colors blend in quiet grace,
Painting love in a sacred space.

The world fades in the softest hue,
As time drips slow, like morning dew.
Reflections calm as waters still,
A gentle pause, a shared will.

We find solace in the night,
Stars above, a guiding light.
With every breath, we feel the bond,
In this quiet, we respond.

Crafting moments with tender care,
A sanctuary where hearts declare.
In the stillness, love's song flows,
In the color of quiet, hope glows.

Where Wildflowers Flourish

In fields where wildflowers sway,
Colors burst in bright array.
Dancing petals in the sun,
Nature sings, a joy begun.

Beneath the sky of azure blue,
Whispers of breezes, soft and true.
Life awakens, blooms so bright,
A tapestry of sheer delight.

Bees hum a gentle serenade,
In this eden, dreams are made.
Each blossom tells a tale untold,
Of secrets woven, hearts unfold.

Passion's hues and joyful cries,
In this garden, love never dies.
Where laughter mingles with the breeze,
Wildflowers flourish, hearts at ease.

Together we roam this fragrant land,
Side by side, hand in hand.
Nature's bounty, a loving embrace,
In wildflower fields, we find our place.

A Mosaic of Eternal Spring

In every petal, stories bloom,
Colors dancing, dispelling gloom.
Seasons blend as dreams take flight,
A mosaic of day and night.

Warmth cascades in golden rays,
Nature's canvas, vibrant displays.
The heart beats to the pulse of time,
In this spring, we feel sublime.

Butterflies flit, a joyful cheer,
In gardens bright, love draws near.
Scented whispers fill the air,
A tapestry of moments rare.

Every heartbeat, every sigh,
Paints a portrait beneath the sky.
Joy unfolds in every scene,
A world awakened, lush and green.

Together we weave this endless song,
In the harmony where we belong.
A mosaic of colors, rich and bold,
In eternal spring, our hearts unfold.

Petal by Petal, Hand in Hand

Petal by petal, we trace the day,
In gentle whispers, we find our way.
Together we step through gardens bright,
Hand in hand, we embrace the light.

Each flower blooms, a tale to share,
As breezes dance with tender care.
In the fragrance of love, we grow,
Nurtured by warmth, our hearts aglow.

Through every storm and sunny sky,
We color the world, just you and I.
Petals flutter in a soft refrain,
Our laughter mingles with the rain.

Roots entwined beneath the ground,
In this embrace, our souls are found.
We rise as one with every dawn,
In the garden where love is born.

Together we weave a vibrant dream,
A tapestry of life, a flowing stream.
Petal by petal, hand in hand,
We nurture love in this sacred land.

Sunlit Strolls in Unity

In the warmth of golden rays,
We wander through the fields of grace.
Hand in hand, we share our days,
With smiles framed on every face.

Beneath the arching trees so tall,
We dance to whispers of the breeze.
Together we shall never fall,
Finding joy in every tease.

The sun dips low, a painted sky,
As laughter lingers in the air.
Each moment passes gently by,
In unity, our spirits flare.

With every step, our hearts align,
In harmony, we leave our trace.
These sunlit paths, forever divine,
In nature's arms, we find our place.

So let us stroll till day is done,
In unity, we'll always thrive.
With each new dawn, our hearts are one,
In this sweet dance, we come alive.

The Harmony of Growth

In gardens lush, we plant our care,
Where seeds of promise find their home.
With patience, love, and tender air,
We nurture dreams and let them roam.

Beneath the sun's embracing light,
Our spirits bloom with vibrant grace.
Through storms and nights of endless fright,
We stand as one in nature's space.

Each sprout a story yet untold,
Together we shall rise and stand.
With hands entwined, our roots grow bold,
United in this sacred land.

As petals unfold, our hearts ignite,
With beauty woven through our days.
In harmony, we find delight,
In every breath, love's sweet array.

Embracing change, we journey on,
In every challenge, we find worth.
Together, stronger, we are drawn,
To foster hope upon this earth.

Nurtured by Nature's Love

Among the trees, we find our peace,
Where rivers sing and mountains rise.
In nature's arms, our souls release,
With wildflowers beneath the skies.

Each dawn unveils a canvas bright,
In colors soft and shadows small.
We wander forth, hearts pure with light,
In nature's love, we stand tall.

With every breeze, new tales arise,
As leaves dance gently overhead.
In gentle whispers, nature sighs,
A lullaby for dreams to spread.

We breathe in deep the fragrant air,
Each heartbeat matches nature's pulse.
In harmony, we shed our care,
A bond that time will never repulse.

So let us roam through fields of green,
With every step, our spirits soar.
In nature's heart, we find the sheen,
Of love that ever will restore.

Flourishing Under the Same Sky

Beneath the vast and endless blue,
We gather 'neath the ancient trees.
In every shade, our friendship grew,
As whispers floated on the breeze.

With laughter ringing through the morn,
We chase the sunlight, hearts aglow.
In unity, we are reborn,
As nature's wonders start to flow.

Each sunset paints our dreams in gold,
A tapestry of shared delight.
With stories bright and futures bold,
We hold the stars within our sight.

In every moment, truths align,
Through seasons' change, our bond won't break.
Together, strong, as we entwine,
In love's embrace, no fear we take.

So let us thrive through every day,
In warmth of light, with spirits high.
Forever blessed, come what may,
Flourishing beneath the same sky.

Togetherness in Every Sprout

In the earth, we sow our dreams,
With tender care, or so it seems.
Together, watch each seedling rise,
A promise held in clear blue skies.

Hands entwined, we water love,
Nurtured by the stars above.
Petals bloom, and hearts entwine,
In every sprout, your hand in mine.

Through storms and sun, we steadfast grow,
In unity, the garden flows.
With every leaf that starts to dance,
We find our strength in sweet romance.

In the breeze, whispers of trust,
From small beginnings, we adjust.
Each sprout a tale of bonds we share,
In every moment, every care.

So let us toil, let love abound,
In every sprout, together found.
The roots of hope, they intertwine,
In every heart, a love divine.

The Symphony of Our Seasons

Spring sings soft, with blooms anew,
A canvas brushed in every hue.
Summer dances in golden rays,
With laughter echoing through the days.

Autumn whispers, leaves descend,
A fiery tale that will not end.
Winter wraps us, cold and bright,
In quiet peace, we share the night.

Each season plays a part, a role,
In the symphony of every soul.
Together, we embrace the change,
Finding beauty in the strange.

With hearts attuned to nature's song,
In every note, we both belong.
Together, we weave time's embrace,
A melody that time won't erase.

So let us dance through every phase,
In life's grand tune, we'll find our ways.
Each season comes as music plays,
In harmony, through all our days.

Field of Shared Dreams

In the meadow, dreams unfold,
A tapestry of tales retold.
Together here, we plant our hopes,
In fields where love and laughter copes.

Beneath the sun, we chase the light,
With every heartbeat, spirits bright.
Each flower blooms, a wish made fair,
In every petal, whispers rare.

Our laughter threads through blades of grass,
In this domain, we boldly pass.
With every breeze, a promise shared,
In dreams and hearts, our souls laid bare.

Through tangled paths, we make our way,
In every step, the colors play.
Together, hand in hand, we roam,
This shared field, our heart's true home.

So let us dance in morning's glow,
In fields where love and wildflowers grow.
As dreams arise, we find our place,
In this embrace, a lasting grace.

Harmony in the Flora

In every bloom, a tale we find,
Of nature's love, beautifully entwined.
Together, gardens flourish bright,
A canvas rich with colors light.

The petals sway, a gentle dance,
In harmony, we take our chance.
With every scent that fills the air,
We breathe in joy, without a care.

With roots connected deep below,
In unity, we come to grow.
Through seasons change, we flourish bold,
In nature's arms, our stories told.

Each leaf a note, each stem a line,
Composing symphonies divine.
Together here, we find our grace,
In the embrace of nature's space.

So let us nurture this sweet refrain,
In harmony, through joy and pain.
Together in the flora's song,
In love's true garden, we belong.

Harmonies in the Soil

In the earth, whispers play,
Life unfolds, night turns to day.
Beneath the surface, secrets dwell,
Songs of the soil, weaves a spell.

Tendrils stretch towards the light,
Each root a dancer, pure delight.
Nature's hymn, a gentle choir,
Breath of the earth, ignites the fire.

In shadows deep, the battles fought,
Hope in every seed that's sought.
From decay, new life shall spring,
Harmonies rise, our voices sing.

Connect the dots, the lines entwine,
In every heart, a story's sign.
Together we grow, in soft embrace,
In the soil, we find our place.

Echoes of time in every grain,
Carried whispers of joy and pain.
In nature's arms, we find the whole,
A symphony alive in the soul.

The Bloom That Binds

Petals open, hearts collide,
In every fragrance, love can't hide.
Colors burst, a vibrant thrill,
Two souls merge, a bond to fill.

In gardens bright, we share our dreams,
A tapestry woven, or so it seems.
Through gentle winds, our hopes take flight,
In every bloom, our hearts ignite.

Roots interlace, the earth does sigh,
Together we grow, reaching high.
With every season, new buds aspire,
In this dance, we're never weary.

Beneath the stars, we find our way,
In moonlit nights, our shadows sway.
With every thorn, a lesson learned,
In every petal, our passion burned.

The bloom that binds, forever shines,
In this garden of intertwining vines.
Each moment savored, love's sweet embrace,
Together we flourish, in this sacred space.

Roots of Connection

Deep in the ground, our roots entwine,
Bound by fate, a love divine.
Through storms we stand, side by side,
In strength, together, we abide.

Branches reaching for the sky,
In moments soft, we learn to fly.
With whispered dreams, our spirits soar,
Roots of connection, forevermore.

Nature's thread, intricately spun,
In quiet moments, we are one.
Every heartbeat a gentle pull,
In the silence, we're never full.

A tapestry woven in shades of trust,
Through time's embrace, we adapt, we rust.
In every season, our love shall bloom,
Lighting the path through whispers of gloom.

From roots of connection, we rise anew,
A sacred dance, just me and you.
Together we grow, in harmony's song,
In every heartbeat, we belong.

Sunlight in Our Embrace

Golden rays touch every face,
Softening shadows, filling space.
In warmth of laughter, hearts ignite,
Sunlight glows, a pure delight.

Together we bask, the day unfolds,
Every moment, a memory holds.
In gentle whispers, secrets shared,
Through trials faced, we have fared.

The warmth of you, a sweet refrain,
In every glance, love's echo reigns.
Through tangled paths, we've found our way,
Sunlight dances, come what may.

With every sunset, dreams set sail,
In twilight's embrace, we shall prevail.
In every heartbeat, our spirits align,
Bathed in sunshine, love's design.

Sunlight in our embrace so true,
In every moment, I cherish you.
Together we flourish, rise and shine,
In love's embrace, forever divine.

A Retreat of Blossoming Hearts

In the meadow where dreams take flight,
Soft whispers dance in the pale moonlight.
Petals unfold, colors bright and fair,
Two souls entwined in a fragrant air.

Time slows down, as laughter rings clear,
Each moment cherished, holding you near.
In this retreat where love finds its voice,
Together we blossom, a beautiful choice.

Seasons may change, yet we'll remain,
In harmony's tune, through joy and pain.
With hearts as gardens, forever we'll bloom,
A retreat of love, dispelling all gloom.

Hand in hand, we weave our own fate,
In this sacred space, we create.
With every heartbeat, we'll nurture this place,
A sanctuary formed from love's embrace.

So here in the garden, we'll pause and reflect,
On every moment, the paths we select.
As blossoms unfurl, so do our dreams,
In this retreat, nothing's as it seems.

The Blooming Hour

As daylight breaks, the blossoms awake,
Colors emerge, in beauty they stake.
Nature sings softly, a sweet serenade,
In this blooming hour, memories are made.

With each gentle breeze, we sway with delight,
Hearts intertwine in the warm morning light.
Petals unfold, like secrets revealed,
In the blooming hour, our fate is sealed.

Time suspends as laughter takes flight,
Every shared glance feels perfectly right.
In this moment, our spirits align,
Entwined in the beauty, your heart next to mine.

The sun drapes softly on fields of gold,
Whispers of love in stories retold.
Together we stand, in nature's embrace,
In this blooming hour, we've found our place.

So let the world pause, as we breathe in,
The magic of the moment, where love can begin.
In the bloom of the hour, our hearts resonate,
A symphony of joy that we create.

Beneath the Blue Sky of Us

Underneath vast skies, so endless and bright,
We lay side by side, hearts dancing in flight.
Clouds drift like whispers, dreams floating high,
In this open space, it's just you and I.

With laughter that bridges each moment we share,
Every beat of our hearts, a love affair.
Together we wander, lost in the blue,
In the most tender moments, just me and you.

The warmth of the sun wraps us in grace,
In the shelter of love, we've found our place.
Beneath the sky's canvas, our spirits unite,
Creating a masterpiece, day into night.

Time drifts like clouds, never rushing away,
Each second a treasure, in our sweet foray.
As stars start to twinkle, the day takes a bow,
Underneath the blue sky, I promise you now.

With dreams in our hearts that forever will stay,
In the glow of the moon, come what may.
Beneath our blue sky, time will not rust,
For in every heartbeat, it's love we trust.

Nature's Embrace of Together

In the woods where the wildflowers grow,
We wander through paths where soft breezes blow.
Nature surrounds us, a tapestry spun,
In her gentle embrace, we're always as one.

The rustle of leaves sings a sweet refrain,
Echoing laughter, intertwining our pain.
With every step, our hearts beat as one,
In nature's embrace, two souls become one.

Amongst the tall trees, time seems to pause,
In the rhythm of life, we hold nature's laws.
The sun filters softly through canopies high,
In the light of your love, I feel I can fly.

As petals fall gently, like whispers of fate,
Each moment we cherish, we truly create.
In this sanctuary, where peace drifts along,
Nature's embrace, our hearts' sweetest song.

So let's linger a while in this tranquil space,
For together we blossom, time leaves not a trace.
In nature's own arms, our spirits soar free,
Forever together, just you and me.

Intermingling Hues of Affection

In the canvas of twilight skies,
Colors dance, as love complies.
Brushstrokes blend, soft and bright,
Creating dreams in morning light.

Hearts entwined like vines they grow,
Through every storm, the love will show.
Whispers shared in quiet night,
Filling shadows with pure light.

Fingers touch, in sweet embrace,
Hues of warmth, love's gentle trace.
Every moment, a work of art,
Crafted slowly, heart to heart.

Time may change the shades we see,
Yet in our hearts, we'll always be.
Vibrant tones that never fade,
In this love, our colors laid.

Together, we paint our bright path,
Merging laughter with love's sweet math.
With every hue that life does lend,
Intermingling, we will transcend.

The Melody of Our Togetherness

In the stillness, your laughter rings,
A sweet tune that my heart sings.
Notes of joy float through the air,
Binding souls with love's sweet care.

Every step we take, in sync,
Our hearts beat close, no time to think.
Dancing through the highs and lows,
In this rhythm, our love grows.

Like a serenade at dusk,
Each whispered word, an echo husk.
Melodies that softly weave,
A tapestry we both believe.

In the silence, notes remain,
A chorus gentle, easing pain.
With every harmony we share,
Together, we breathe vibrant air.

So let us play this song so true,
A symphony of me and you.
In every phrase, our spirits soar,
The melody that we adore.

Whispers Among the Petals

Among the blooms, we softly tread,
Where secrets and sweet dreams are spread.
Petals rustle with every sigh,
In whispers, our spirits fly.

A garden lush where feelings grow,
With every touch, feelings glow.
Breezes carry our gentle words,
Like songs of sweet, unseen birds.

Sunrise paints the blossoms bright,
Every hue a pure delight.
In this beauty, we find our way,
Guided by love, come what may.

In still moments, our hearts discern,
Lessons in the love we learn.
Each petal holds a promise true,
Whispers shared, just me and you.

So as we wander, hand in hand,
Through this fragrant, vibrant land,
Let our whispers softly blend,
Among the petals, love won't end.

Blossoms of Our Togetherness

In the spring, new life awakes,
Among the blooms, our love heart aches.
Petals open to the warm embrace,
Revealing joy in every space.

Together we cultivate our dreams,
In sunlight's glow, our laughter beams.
Roots entwined in fertile ground,
In each other's love, we are found.

With every season, we take flight,
Through storms and days both dark and bright.
Blossoms whisper truths so clear,
In the garden, love draws near.

Colors burst in vibrant show,
As time unfolds, our love will grow.
In fragrant blooms, our souls align,
In this dance, forever entwined.

So let us cherish every bloom,
And find our home in love's sweet room.
With each flower, one thing is true,
In all blossoms, I choose you.

Whispers in the Wind

Gentle breezes call my name,
Secrets woven, never tame.
Leaves are dancing, soft, and light,
Carrying dreams into the night.

Stars above, they quietly gleam,
Painting shadows, living dream.
Whispers float, through trees they wend,
Nature's voice, our hearts contend.

Moonlit paths invite us close,
A symphony of love, morose.
Hands entwined beneath the sky,
Where echoes fade and wishes fly.

Fingers trace the ancient bark,
In the stillness, we embark.
Time drips slowly, like the dew,
In every breath, I find you true.

With each gust a promise made,
In the silence, fears will fade.
Whispers in the wind, so sweet,
In our hearts, two souls can meet.

Unfurling Hearts Together

Beneath the sun, we find our space,
In each other, we embrace.
With every glance, our spirits soar,
Unfurling love, forever more.

Silken petals, soft and bright,
Colors blending, pure delight.
Together growing, roots entwined,
Hearts in rhythm, love defined.

Through stormy nights and sunny days,
We dance in life's unpredictable ways.
Hand in hand, we face the test,
In our union, we find rest.

Dreams unfurling like the dawn,
In every moment, we are drawn.
With laughter ringing, skies so clear,
Together flowing, year by year.

And as the seasons come and go,
In fertile soil, our love will grow.
Unfurling hearts, a sacred trust,
In this journey, love is a must.

Seeds of Together

In the garden where we meet,
Planting dreams beneath our feet.
Each small seed, a wish to share,
In the soil, we lay our care.

Sunlight warms the gentle ground,
Whispers of our hopes abound.
Nurtured hearts in quiet strife,
Growing roots, entwined in life.

With every rain, our fears subside,
In this garden, we confide.
Blooming brightly, colors yield,
Seeds of love in nature's field.

Time will pass, and seasons change,
Yet our bond will not feel strange.
Together always, side by side,
In the harvest, hearts abide.

Seeds of together, strong and bold,
Telling stories yet untold.
In the quiet, visions thrive,
In this space, our love's alive.

A Love Rooted in Nature

In the forest, our hearts align,
Through ancient trees, love's design.
Whispers linger in the air,
A connection beyond compare.

Roots dig deep in fertile earth,
In this bond, we find our worth.
Branches stretch to skies above,
Cradling dreams, a testament of love.

Flowers bloom in vibrant hues,
Painting paths of reds and blues.
Each petal holds a story shared,
Promises made and hopes declared.

Rain will fall and sun will rise,
Mirrored in your loving eyes.
Nature sings, a soothing sound,
In your arms, my peace is found.

A love rooted, strong and true,
In every season, ever new.
Together thriving, side by side,
In nature's embrace, we abide.

A Canvas of Green Dreams

Whispers of leaves on a gentle breeze,
A tapestry woven with vibrant trees.
Sunlight dances on emerald hues,
In this realm where nature renews.

Birdsongs flutter in the morning light,
Glades of peace in the soft twilight.
Each petal painted with love's own hand,
A world of wonder, serene and grand.

Streams that giggle and waters that hum,
In this lush haven, my heart feels at home.
Beneath the boughs, dreams softly sway,
In the canvas of green where I'm lost each day.

Clouds drift softly, shadows embrace,
The pulse of the earth in a tranquil space.
Here I wander, a soul in flight,
In a sanctuary of pure delight.

Nature's fond canvas, forever gleams,
A sanctuary painted with whispering dreams.
Every corner fulfilling a wish,
In this verdant paradise—my heart's tryst.

Blossoming Beneath the Stars

In the moonlight's glow, petals unfold,
Stories of love in secrets told.
Dreams take flight on fragrant air,
We dance together without a care.

Stars twinkle down, a celestial show,
Lighting the world where sweet flowers grow.
The rhythm of night, a soft serenade,
In this garden, memories are made.

Soft whispers flow like a gentle stream,
Wrapped in magic, we share a dream.
The night blooms bright with a dazzling cheer,
In this moment, everything feels near.

Petals shimmer with the morning dew,
A tapestry woven of me and you.
Together we flourish, hearts intertwined,
In the night sky, our love is enshrined.

Beneath the stars, our souls ignite,
In a melody sweet, a world of light.
Through blooming gardens, we find our way,
In the darkest hours, love leads the day.

Echoes of Earthbound Love

In autumn's embrace, leaves softly fall,
Whispers of time in nature's call.
The scent of earth after summer's glow,
Tales of love in the warm breezes flow.

Each moment captured in sunlight's kiss,
A dance of shadows, a fleeting bliss.
Hand in hand, through forests we roam,
Together we create our sacred home.

The mountains echo with laughter and song,
In the heart of nature, where we belong.
The rivers murmur as they meander near,
In every heartbeat, I feel you here.

Under starlit skies, we find our way,
The cosmos whispers what words can't say.
Traces of you linger on the breeze,
In every rustle of the dancing trees.

Our love, a compass in the quiet night,
Guides us forward with a gentle light.
In this earthbound song, forever we stay,
Where echoes of love lead us day by day.

Together in Bloom

Under the sun, blossoms unveil,
In colors that tell a wondrous tale.
Together we stand, hand in hand,
In a world of joy, steady and grand.

Petals whisper secrets, soft and sweet,
In the garden's heart, our souls meet.
With every new dawn, we begin anew,
Bound in the magic of vibrant hue.

The fragrance of spring fills the air,
In the dance of flowers, love is rare.
Each moment cherished, a promise true,
In every bloom, I find a piece of you.

As seasons change, our roots run deep,
In the soil of memories, together we keep.
Through storms and sunshine, we persevere,
In a blossoming bond, forever near.

Together in bloom, a love so divine,
In this garden of dreams, your heart's in mine.
Through petals and time, forever we soar,
In the embrace of nature, we bloom evermore.

The Leafy Embrace

In the woodland's depth, I roam,
With leaves like whispers, I find home.
Their gentle rustle, a soft caress,
Nature's heart, a sweet confess.

Sunlight dapples through the trees,
Brushing softly, a tender breeze.
Each leaf a story, old and wise,
Beneath the branches, my spirit flies.

Ferns and petals weave a quilt,
A tapestry of life, finely built.
In every shade, a secret resides,
In leafy embrace, the world abides.

The rhythm of life, a sacred song,
In this green haven, I belong.
Moments linger, time stands still,
In nature's arms, I feel the thrill.

Underneath the ancient boughs,
I breathe in peace, I make my vows.
To cherish all that life bestows,
In leafy embrace, my garden grows.

Interlaced Threads of Nature

A spider weaves with care and grace,
Threads of silver, a hidden space.
In morning's light, a dance appears,
Nature's craft, captured years.

Flowers bloom in colors bright,
A canvas painted with pure delight.
Each petal holds a drop of dew,
In vibrant hues, the world feels new.

Birds aloft on whispered air,
Songs of freedom, without a care.
They interlace the azure skies,
With each note, my spirit flies.

Roots run deep beneath the soil,
Interwoven lives, they toil.
Connected by a hidden thread,
In nature's web, where all are led.

Together we thrive, hand in hand,
In unity, we take our stand.
Interlaced threads creating one,
In nature's heart, we are all spun.

Vibrant Footprints on Soft Earth

Across the meadow, gently tread,
With vibrant footprints, forward spread.
Each step a mark, a tale to tell,
In the soft earth, where memories dwell.

The colors splash where wildflowers grow,
In every corner, life will show.
A dance of hues under the sun,
In vibrant steps, we feel as one.

Nature's canvas, textured and bright,
Our footprints linger, a joyful sight.
With every stride, we leave our trace,
In a world embraced, we find our place.

Listen closely, the earth does speak,
In whispers gentle and sometimes meek.
It marks our journey, both far and near,
With vibrant footprints, we persevere.

So let us wander, let us explore,
Each step unfolding, life's open door.
With every imprint, a story made,
On soft earth's fabric, our dreams cascade.

The Beauty of Togetherness

In every gathering, hearts ignite,
A bond that glows, a shared delight.
With laughter's echo, spirits rise,
In the beauty of togetherness, we find the skies.

Hands entwined in moments rare,
Companions present, a love laid bare.
Each voice a melody, soft and true,
In this symphony, I cherish you.

Through storms we stand, in bright embrace,
Strength in unity, we hold our space.
With trust as our anchor, hope our sail,
In the beauty of togetherness, we shall prevail.

Seasons change, yet we remain,
A legacy of joy, beyond the pain.
Together we build, together we mend,
In the beauty of togetherness, we transcend.

So let us gather, let us sing,
In this dance of life, joy we bring.
Hand in hand, through thick and thin,
In the beauty of togetherness, we begin.

Beneath the Vines of Connection

Beneath the vines we find our way,
Tangled roots where dreams hold sway.
In quiet moments, laughter rings,
Among the leaves, our spirit sings.

The sun peeks through, a golden ray,
Illuminating words we say.
With every step, the past we trace,
In nature's arms, we find our place.

The whispers of the wind do call,
In twilight's glow, we stand tall.
Through winding paths and shadows cast,
We weave our stories, unsurpassed.

The rustle speaks of bonds so deep,
In vibrant shades, our secrets keep.
Beneath the vines, we grow and learn,
In every twist, our hearts discern.

Together here, we carve our fate,
With open hearts, we celebrate.
In every leaf, a tale unfolds,
Beneath the vines, our love beholds.

The Reluctant Bloom

A bud in shadows, fears tucked tight,
Hesitant to greet the morning light.
Whispers of spring evoke a sigh,
Yearning for wings but too shy to fly.

The chill of doubt wraps me in chains,
Yet deep within, a courage gains.
In silent moments, a spark ignites,
A call to dance in the soft moonlight.

With gentle warmth, the sun does tease,
Encouraging hope to seize the breeze.
Petals unfold, revealing grace,
In every color, I find my place.

The reluctant bloom, with heart aglow,
Embraces the peace that starts to grow.
In harmony, I share my tune,
No longer bound, I blossom soon.

With every struggle, strength has grown,
In vibrant hues, love has sown.
The reluctant bloom, now bold and bright,
Finds joy in the embrace of light.

Whispering Promises in Full Bloom

In gardens rich with whispers sweet,
Promises dance on petals neat.
A symphony of colors play,
Telling stories in their sway.

Butterflies drift in a gentle waltz,
Tracing dreams where the heart exalts.
Each fragrant sigh, a vow to keep,
In tender moments that make us leap.

Beneath the boughs, our laughter rings,
A chorus of joy that brightly sings.
In morning's glow, our hands entwined,
Whispered secrets, two hearts aligned.

Every petal holds a timeless spark,
A memory cast in shadows dark.
With each breeze, our hopes take flight,
In gardens vast, we chase the light.

Together we flourish, blooms in hand,
Whispering promises across the land.
In full bloom, our spirits soar,
In nature's heart, we yearn for more.

Together in Nature's Care

In nature's cradle, hand in hand,
We wander softly, lost in the land.
With every footprint in the earth,
We plant our hopes, we share our worth.

The babbling brooks, they guide our way,
As sunlight spills at end of day.
Amidst the trees, we find our song,
Together where we both belong.

Each rustling leaf holds a secret dear,
In every sigh, we draw near.
Nature speaks in whispers low,
Uniting hearts with all it shows.

In twilight's grasp, the stars emerge,
As dreams awaken, thoughts converge.
Underneath the vast expanse,
In unity, we take our chance.

Together in this sacred space,
Embracing every trace and grace.
In nature's care, we thrive and grow,
With love as deep as rivers flow.